5. 1
0. 5

READING POWER

Famous American Trails

The Mormon Pioneer Trail

From Nauvoo, Illinois, to the Great Salt Lake, Utah

Arlan Dean

The Rosen Publishing Group's
PowerKids Press™
New York

Published in 2003 by The Rosen Publishing Group, Inc.
29 East 21st Street, New York, NY 10010

First Edition

Book Design: Christopher Logan

Photo Credits: Cover courtesy of the Union Pacific Historical Collection (cover image has been digitally enhanced with permission); p. 4 Print Collection, Miriam and Ira D. Wallach Division of Art, The New York Public Library, Astor, Lenox and Tilden Foundations; p. 5 Missouri State Archives Mormon War Papers Collection; p. 6 "Saints Driven from Jackson County" by C.C.A. Christensen, courtesy of the Brigham Young University Museum of Art; pp. 7 (top), 13 (inset), 14–15, 18–19 © Hulton/Archive/Getty Images; p. 7 (bottom) Irma and Paul Milstein Division of United States History, Local History and Genealogy, The New York Public Library, Astor, Lenox and Tilden Foundations; pp. 8–9 Library of Congress, Prints and Photographs Division; p. 9 (map) Christopher Logan; p. 10 "Winter Quarters" by C.C.A. Christensen, courtesy of the Brigham Young University Museum of Art; p. 11 L. Tom Perry Special Collections, Harold B. Lee Library, Brigham Young University, Provo, Utah, photograph by Anderson; pp. 12–13 Special Collections, J. Willard Marriott Library, University of Utah; p. 14 (inset) courtesy of the Denver Public Library, Western History Collection, X-11929; pp. 16, 17, 20, 21 © Dan Guravich; p. 18 (inset) © North Wind Picture Archives

Library of Congress Cataloging-in-Publication Data

Dean, Arlan.
The Mormon pioneer trail : from Nauvoo, Illinois to the Great Salt
Lake, Utah / Arlan Dean.
   p. cm. — (Famous American trails)
Summary: The story of the Mormon Trail and the migration of Mormons to their new settlement at Salt Lake City.
Includes bibliographical references and index.
ISBN 0-8239-6476-0 (lib. bdg.)
1. Mormon Pioneer National Historic Trail—History—Juvenile literature. 2. Mormon pioneers—West (U.S.)—History—Juvenile literature. 3. Frontier and pioneer life—West (U.S.)—Juvenile literature. 4. West (U.S.)—History—19th century—Juvenile literature. [1. Mormon Pioneer National Historic Trail. 2. Mormons—History.] I. Title.
F593 .D29 2003
978—dc21

2002000125

Contents

The Need for a Better Life

The Mormons had different religious beliefs than other people. Many people disliked them because of their different beliefs.

Joseph Smith

The Mormons belonged to The Church of Latter Day Saints. The church was started in New York State by Joseph Smith, the son of a farmer, in 1830.

Mormons were often forced to move from their homes by other people. The Mormons moved from state to state, looking for places where they could live safely.

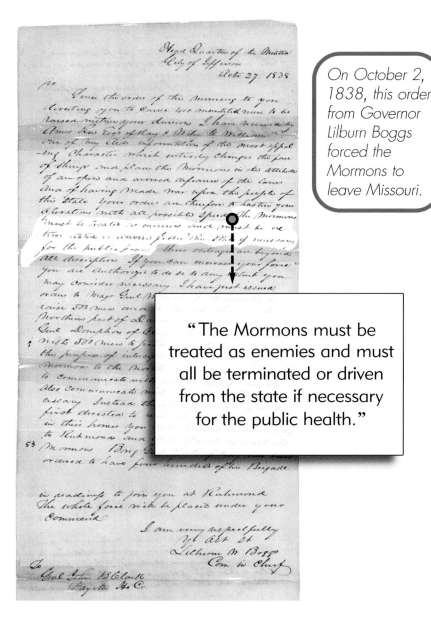

On October 2, 1838, this order from Governor Lilburn Boggs forced the Mormons to leave Missouri.

"The Mormons must be treated as enemies and must all be terminated or driven from the state if necessary for the public health."

In 1839, Joseph Smith led the Mormons from Missouri to Illinois. In Illinois, they built the city of Nauvoo. However, the Mormons were not able to enjoy Nauvoo for long.

Check It Out

Nauvoo means "beautiful" in the Hebrew language.

Nauvoo

In 1844, Smith had trouble with his enemies and was put in jail in the nearby town of Carthage, Illinois. An angry group of people went to the jail and killed him. Brigham Young became the new leader of the Mormons.

Brigham Young

Carthage jail

The Mormon Pioneer Trail

In 1846, Young decided to guide the Mormons westward in search of a new home. His group followed a path that would become known as the Mormon Pioneer Trail.

Check It Out

The Mormon Pioneer Trail went from Nauvoo, Illinois, to the Great Salt Lake in Utah. It crossed through five states and covered more than 1,200 miles.

THE MORMON PIONEER TRAIL

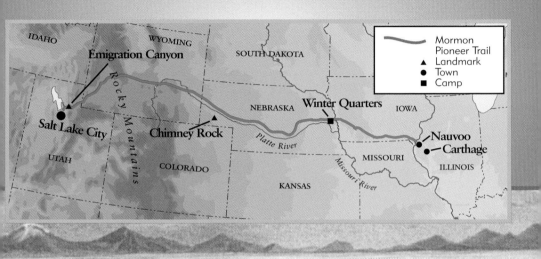

The Great Salt Lake, Utah

On Their Way

After four months of traveling, Young and about 5,000 Mormons arrived at the Missouri River. They built a camp called Winter Quarters. While there, Young made plans to move the Mormon people to the Great Salt Lake Valley in Utah.

Check It Out

More than 600 Mormons died of illnesses or accidents during their stay at Winter Quarters.

Winter Quarters

Many Mormon children traveled along the Mormon Pioneer Trail with their families.

In 1847, Young led a small group of Mormon pioneers from Winter Quarters to the Great Salt Lake Valley.

Brigham Young's Pioneer Company

In Brigham Young's small group there were 143 men, 3 women, 2 children, 72 wagons, 93 horses, 66 oxen, 52 mules, 19 cows, 17 dogs, and some chickens.

The group followed the Platte River west until they came to the Rocky Mountains. Then, they crossed the mountains and finally came to the Great Salt Lake Valley.

The Great Salt Lake Valley

The Mormons had to cross the Platte River on their way to the Great Salt Lake Valley.

This Mormon family packed all of their belongings in two wagons for their trip to the West.

Soon, thousands of Mormons were making the long journey west along the Mormon Pioneer Trail. Mormons from as far away as Europe traveled the trail. Some people traveled by wagon, and others walked, pulling handcarts.

Handcarts were pulled by people, not animals. Handcarts were a cheap way for people with little money to travel. Each handcart could hold up to 500 pounds of supplies.

Life on the Trail

The Mormons woke early each morning to begin the day's journey on the trail. They improved the trail as they traveled because they knew that other Mormons would soon follow them.

Chimney Rock

Chimney Rock in Nebraska was a famous landmark along the trail. As settlers passed the rock, they knew they were at the end of the prairie and heading into the mountains.

The Mormons cleared paths and marked trails so people would have an easier time traveling.

A Well-Stocked Wagon

Every family making the journey along the Mormon Pioneer Trail was given a supply list. Important supplies included:

1,000 lbs. of flour, 100 lbs. of sugar, 20 lbs. of soap, 15 lbs. of iron and steel, 10 lbs. of rice, 2 or 3 oxen, 2 or more milk cows, and 1 good wagon.

To mark their trip on the Mormon Pioneer Trail, many people cut their names into rocks along the way.

The journey to the Great Salt Lake Valley was not easy and often unsafe. One group of Mormons was caught in a blizzard in the Rocky Mountains.

Buffalo stampedes were always a danger for travelers on the Mormon Pioneer Trail.

Many of them died of cold and hunger before a group of Mormons from the Great Salt Lake Valley could save them.

Check It Out

From 1846 to 1869, more than 70,000 Mormons traveled across the United States on the Mormon Pioneer Trail.

The Trail Today

The Mormon Pioneer Trail was important in opening up the West for new settlers. In 1978, the United States government made the Mormon Pioneer Trail part of its National Trail System. This historic trail honors the journey of the thousands of brave Mormons who traveled west in search of religious freedom.

Today, wagon tracks can still be seen on the Mormon Pioneer Trail. These tracks are on part of the trail in Wyoming.

This monument in Utah's Pioneer Trail State Park honors the Mormon pioneers and others who traveled to the West.

The Mormon Pioneer Trail Time Line

1830	The Mormon Church is started by Joseph Smith in New York State.
1839	The Mormons move from Missouri to Illinois.
1844	Joseph Smith is killed in Carthage, Illinois. Brigham Young becomes the leader of the Mormon Church.
1846	Mormons are made to leave Nauvoo.
1846–1847	Mormons live at Winter Quarters in present-day Nebraska.
1847	Brigham Young leads a small group of Mormons to the Great Salt Lake Valley.
1846–1869	More than 70,000 Mormons travel along the trail to the Great Salt Lake Valley.
1978	The Mormon Pioneer Trail becomes part of the U.S. government's National Trail System.

Glossary

blizzard (**blihz**-uhrd) a snowstorm with very strong, icy winds

company (**kuhm**-puh-nee) a group of people joined together for some purpose

enemies (**ehn**-uh-meez) people who hate and try to harm each other

Great Salt Lake (**grayt sawlt layk**) a large saltwater lake located in the state of Utah

handcarts (**hand**-kartz) small, hand-pulled wagons with two wheels

Mormon (**mor**-muhn) a member of the church started by Joseph Smith

pioneer (py-uh-**nihr**) someone who goes first to prepare a way for other people

prairie (**prair**-ee) a large area of flat land that is covered with grass and has few or no trees

stampedes (stam-**peedz**) when large groups of animals run together suddenly

terminated (**tehr**-muh-nay-tuhd) to have been ended or come to an end

Resources

Books

American Kids in History: Pioneer Days
by David C. King
John Wiley & Sons (1997)

Brigham Young: Mormon and Pioneer
by Charnan Simon
Children's Press (1999)

Web Sites

Due to the changing nature of Internet links, PowerKids Press has developed an on-line list of Web sites related to the subjects of this book. This site is updated regularly. Please use this link to access the list:

http://www.powerkidslinks.com/fat/mort/

Index

Word Count: 479

Note to Librarians, Teachers, and Parents

If reading is a challenge, Reading Power is a solution! Reading Power is perfect for readers who want high-interest subject matter at an accessible reading level. These fact-filled, photo-illustrated books are designed for readers who want straightforward vocabulary, engaging topics, and a manageable reading experience. With clear picture/text correspondence, leveled Reading Power books put the reader in charge. Now readers have the power to get the information they want and the skills they need in a user-friendly format.